Igor
STRAVINSKY

THE FIREBIRD
(L'OISEAU DE FEU)
1919 SUITE, K 10c

Edited by
Clark McAlister
Clinton F. Nieweg

Study Score
Partitur

SERENISSIMA MUSIC, INC.

CONTENTS

1. Introduction 1

2. L'oiseau de feu et sa danse 6

3. Variation de l'oiseu de feu 7

4. Ronde de Princesses 19

5. Danse infernale du roi Katscheï 27

6. Berceuse.. 74

7. Final... 79

Previously issued by E.F. Kalmus as A2131. The large conductor's score
and matching orchestral parts are also available from
Serenissima Music, Inc.

SOURCES and NOTES

Ballet Full Scores:
Manuscript facsimile of the Complete Ballet. Geneva: Conservatoire de Musique, 1985.
Études et commentaries par Louis Cyr, Jean-Jacques Eigeldinger, Pierre Wissmer. 35 x 46 cm, 167, 61 pp.
Moscow: P. Jurgenson, (1910). Plate 34920, 180 pp. - assigned to Schott in 1933 (Europe)
Reprint: New York: E.F. Kalmus, n.d. [1933-75]
Reprint: Miami: Edwin F. Kalmus, n.d.[1975 onward]. Catalog A3049
London: Eulenburg, Preface ©1996. Critical Ballet Score: Schott/EU 8043 [parts on rental]
Moscow: Muzyka, 1964. 172 pp.
Reprint: Mineola: Dover Publications, 1987. [No parts published]

1911 Full Score:
Moscow: P. Jurgenson, (1911). Plate 35965, 98 pp.
Reprint: Boca Raton: Edwin F. Kalmus, n.d.[1975 onward]. Catalog A 2132

1919 Full Scores:
Composer's Manuscript (ms.) archived at BnF, Bibliothèque nationale France. Code: RES VMA MS-8
London: J. &. W. Chester, Ltd. ©1920. Plate J.W.C. 17, 79 pp.
Reprint: New York: Edwin F. Kalmus, 1932. Kalmus miniature orchestra scores, No. 41 [Later Belwin, Alfred]
Reprint: New York: Edwin F. Kalmus, No. 41 (marked copy)
Leonard Bernstein marked score and parts. [New York Philharmonic Archives, ID:2330]
Reprint: New York: Boosey & Hawkes, n.d.[1940 onward]. B. & H. No. 573
Boca Raton: Edwin F. Kalmus, ©1985, 1989. Edited Clark McAlister, Catalog A 2131.
Extensively corrected reprint of the 1920 Chester full score above.
"To try to capitalize on an existing copyright score, Stravinsky made a new suite of The Firebird for reduced orchestra [1919] and sold
it, illicitly as it turned out, to his new London publisher, J. & W. Chester. The first performance was conducted by Ernest Ansermet in
Geneva, Victoria-Hall, April 12, 1919."[1]

1919 Parts:
London: J. &. W. Chester, Ltd. ©1920. Plate J.W.C. 17
Reprint: New York: Edwin F. Kalmus, n.d.[1933-1984]
There are some minor differences / corrections from the original Chester publication
Boca Raton: Edwin F. Kalmus, ©1985, 1989. Edited Clark McAlister, Catalog A 2131.
Extensively corrected reprint of the 1920 Chester parts above.

1945 Study Score:
New York: Leeds Music Corp., 1947, 117 pp. (assigned to MCA, Inc. 1973)
Reprint: London: Eulenburg. Preface ©1982 Schott. No. EU 1389 [1945 suite parts on rental]
"Robert Craft writes that Stravinsky created the 1945 suite by consulting not his own Ballet manuscript, but rather the Kalmus
reprint of the Chester score available in the U.S. at the time."[2]

Piano Reduction (original): Moscow: P. Jurgenson, (July 1911). Plates 34903-34919, 66 pp.
Reprint: New York: G. Schirmer, n.d.(ca.1915)
Reprint: Mineola: Dover Publications, 2006
Piano Reduction (revised): Mainz: Schott Musik International ©1936 ED 3279, 70 pp.
A second version of the piano reduction was completed 6 December 1918 and dedicated to Vladimir Vasilievich Yuzhin.
The manuscript of the first version and an annotated proof of the second are in the Pierpont Morgan Library, New York.[3]

The Kirchmeyer catalog gives extensive details about all publications of *Firebird* in chapter K010.[4]

Except for changing the instrumentation there are sections of the 1919 suite that are taken directly from the ballet. In those sections corrections in
articulations, dynamics and bowings in the 2016 edition are notated as in the ballet manuscript. In other sections the 1919 suite was completely re-
orchestrated. In those sections corrections in articulations, dynamics, and bowings are notated from the parts and other sources.

In the *Danse Infernale du roi Kastcheï* three measures of the trumpets and trombones have pitches printed in the 1919 suite that are not the same as
the pitches printed in the ballet. See the Table of Major Discrepancies below, in measures 210, 214, 220, for the research about the different notes in
the editions. Also consult the Orchestra Music Errata Catalog.[5]

This edition has been newly engraved with reference to the previously corrected 1919 scores; the ballet score, the 1945 score and the original engraved orchestral parts. The new engraving has measure numbers notated, with boxed measure numbers where the 1919 Chester score has rehearsal
numbers. It is the first new engraving of this work, a major one on the concert repertoire, in nearly a century.

Clinton F. Nieweg, August, 2016

[1] Stephen Walsh, <http://paideiamusical.blogspot.com/2009/10/igor-stravinsky-1882-1971.html>
[2] Vera Stravinsky, Robert Craft, ed., *Stravinsky in Pictures and Documents 378. 15* (Simon and Schuster, 1979)
[3] Robert Craft, ed., Stravinsky: Selected Correspondence, Vol. II. (New York: Alfred A. Knopf, 1985)
[4] Helmut Kirchmeyer, ed., "Chapter K010" Annotated Catalog of Works and Work Editions of Igor Strawinsky till 1971,
K Catalog, January 2014, <www.kcatalog.org>
[5] Orchestra Music Errata Catalog, Clinton F. Nieweg / Nancy M. Bradburd errata lists, dated 10 / 2008 & 4 / 2009. MOLA-inc.org

TABLE OF MAJOR DISCREPANCIES
Textual Notes

ABBREVIATIONS: Status codes: ! - is critical; would stop rehearsal. s/r = should read. M. = measure. R.H. = Right Hand. L.H. = Left Hand. U, M, L = upper, middle, or lower line of a divisi section. [ ] = editorial decision. - Dash = to. Example: 10 - 14 = measures 10 to 14. , Comma = and. Example: 10, 14 = measures 10 and 14. ? = A change to be made at the conductor's discretion. ms. = Stravinsky's 1919 autograph manuscript.

NOTE: As in the original engraving, cues in the parts are in the transposition of the cued instrument.

Status Code	Inst.	Meas. No.	Beat	Comment
				Introduction
	Basses	1		Stand 1 Basses plays *pizz. senza sord.* per the part layout and the ballet. Stand 1 adds the mute at measure 14.
	Tutti	7, 8		No dotted lines to divide the measures are shown in the ms. for measure 7 and 8. The dotted lines are in the ms. in measure 12.
	Horn I, II	13	1	In the 1919 ms. a *sf* dynamic is shown above the staff for Horn 1 and *sfp* below the staff for Horn II. Both are stopped.
?	Violin I	14, 15		The Violin I scordatura glissando can be handled in three ways: 1. Perform the gliss. as presented in the ballet and 1911 suite (without re-tuning) starting on the D string sounding D6, an octave higher than the Violin 2. Within the gliss, the pitches will be slightly different, but the effect will be very similar to the ballet and no retuning is necessary. The first note would be fingered as the 1st harmonic on the D-string. Notated in the 2016 edition. 2. Play the gliss. starting on the D string sounding D5, in the same octave as the Violin 2, though displaced rhythmically by one 8th-note as notated in the 1919 ms, original Chester score and the 1945 score. Within the gliss, the pitches will be correct, but in the same octave as Violin 2. Remove the now superfluous notation "Tune the E string to D." The 1919 ms. has an arrow up and then an arrow down under each 4 notes. 3. Play the gliss. on the re-tuned E string, starting on D6 sounding an octave higher than the Violin 2, as notated in the ballet and 1911 suite. Conductor decision.
?	E.H.	23	1, 2	This is the only measure with E.H. in the 1919 suite. Many conductors have this measure played on Oboe. The 2016 edition includes a transposed version of the E.H. measure in the Oboe II and Oboe I part.
				Variation de l'oiseau de feu
	Tutti	39 etc.		The 2016 edition adds dynamics to conform with the ballet.
	Cl. I	39	2, 3	No accents appear in any ballet edition. While accents were printed with each beat in the old Chester edition, the 2016 edition deletes these accents to conform to the ballet editions.
	Strings	53	1	The *pizz.* chord is notated as a dotted quarter in the 1919 ms. Eighth note used in the 2016 edition as notated in the ballet ms. and corrected by I.S. in the 1945 score. See measure 55 beat 1 in the 1919 suite which has an eight note. No audible difference.
	Fl. I	59	3 - 6	The Flute passage was incorrectly transposed and engraved for 1st Clarinet in the original 1919 Chester edition. Corrected in the 1989 publication, per the ballet pitches. No accents in the 2016 edition.

!	Tutti	68 to 72		The *sempre crescendo* (in ballet *poco a poco crescendo*) is printed as a continuous four measure *crescendo* from *p* to *f* in measure 72. The 2016 edition eliminates the drop to *p* in measure 70 found in previous editions, to create the continuous four measure *crescendo*.
?	Tutti	72, 73	1, 2	The 1919 score printed *dim.* signs. The ballet manuscript and printed score have *cresc.* signs. See measure 76. Did I.S. change his idea for the 1919 and 1945 suites, or did the engraver read the 1919 manuscript incorrectly? The 2016 edition uses the ballet dynamics.
!	Bsn. I	72, 73	3	First note of the triplet: Piano reduction and ballet has A-nat. in Flute. The Bassoon rests. 1919 engraved G-nat. (*sic*). 1945 score has F-nat. 2016 corrected to A-nat. an octave below the Flute.
!	Piano, Harp	80, 81	1	The 1919 Chester score, 1989 reprint and 2016 edition notates "open ties" on these final chords for the notes to *Laisser vibrer*, while the rest of the orchestra plays a short note.
				Ronde des princesses
!	Viola	50	3	The ballet, original 1919 suite and piano reduction have a B-natural throughout this measure (half note tied to quarter). The 1945 suite has an A-sharp on the third beat. The 2016 edition restores the original sustained B-natural.
!	Violin I, Upper Cello	95	1+	The second note of this meas. is A-(nat.) in the piano reduction, in the ballet and the original 1919 suite score and parts. The note was marked A-sharp by Leonard Bernstein in the parts (but not in his score). The WW play A-sharp. A-nat. notated in the 2016 edition.
				Danse infernale du roi Kastcheï
	Bsn, Hn., Tuba	4, 6, 8, 12, 14, 16	3	Beat 3 has a quarter note in the ballet. In the 1919 suite there is a mix of quarter and eighth note rhythms. 2016 edition conforms to the ballet notation.
	Flute, Picc.	11	1 etc.	In the ballet the grace notes are engraved before beat 1. The 1919 suite and 2016 edition have the grace notes engraved on beat 1.
	Tuba	14	2+, 3	The 2016 edition adds E to E-flat in Tuba as in the ballet Reh. 133 meas. 6, and 1945 suite Reh. 89 meas. 4. The original engraving of the 1919 suite is missing this entrance.
	Harp	47	1	*p* is engraved in the 1919 suite. The 2016 edition uses *f* as corrected in the 1945 suite for better balance.
	Harp	66		The ballet and 1945 suite repeats measure 65 8va in measure 66. The 1919 suite is missing the notes in measure 66. The 2016 edition conforms with the ballet and 1945 suite.
	Flute I	83, 89, 90	3+	The ballet, 1919 ms. and 2016 edition notate the grace notes a half step lower than beat 2+. The 1919 engraving has incorrect pitches.
	Violin I, II	89, 90	2+, 3+	In the 2016 edition, the chords are notated as in the ballet and the 1919 ms.; I.S. wrote pizz. and an arpeggio sign with an up arrow.
	Tutti	91 - 96		WW, Strs. *ff sempre* in the ballet. *ff cresc.* in the 1945 suite. WW who previously are at *ff,* have no beginning dynamic, then *cresc.* in the 1919 suite. 2016 edition uses the ballet notation.
?	Viola	101		Original 1919 Chester score: B♭–A♭, A♭-G♭, G♭-F | Original 1919 Chester part: B♭–A♭, A♭-G♭, **E♭-D♭** | Chester score used by Bernstein: B♭–A♭, A♭-G♭, G♭-F | Chester part changed by Bernstein: B♭–A♭, **G♭-F,** E♭-D♭ | Kalmus 1989 publication & 1945 suite: B♭-A♭, A♭-G♭, **G♭-A♭** | Orchestration different in the ballet.

				2016 edition notates B♭-A♭, A♭-G♭, **F-E♭**
!	Bsn. I	108	1	Original 1919 suite Chester score has B-flat. Original Chester part C-flat. No B-flat in the chord in the ballet or the piano reduction. 2016 edition notates C-flat like the 1945 suite and 1919 part.
?	Bass	129, 131, 133 etc. to 139		Original 1919 Chester and 1945 score have a short cresc. sign on beat 1. Another cresc. starts on beat 1+ into the next measure. This pattern continues to measure 140. 2016 edition uses a cresc. on the dotted quarter note.
!	Timp.	189, 191	1	Notes missing in the 1919 score. Ballet notates D-sharp. 1945 suite notates A. 2016 edition uses the ballet notation.
!	Timp.	201 to 208	1	The 1919 ms. and Chester score have the notes as low E. The 2016 edition notates A as in the ballet, 1945 suite and 1989 reprint.
!	Tpt. II	210, 214	4	1919 and 1945 suites notate A-nat. The piano reduction chord has D, F-sharp, G-sharp. The ballet at Reh. 171 for Tpt. I has G-sharp. A-flat for Tpt II notated in the 2016 edition.
!	Tpt. II	220	1	Original 1919 and 1945 suites have A-nat. The piano reduction chord at Reh. 174 meas. 4, has F-nat., G-sharp, B-nat. Orchestra chord has an A-flat. B-nat. notated in the 2016 edition.
!	Tbn. III	220	1	Original 1919 and 1945 suites notate F-sharp. Piano reduction chord at Reh. 173 has F-nat., G-sharp, B-nat. Ballet Reh. 173 meas. 4 has F-nat. which is notated in the 2016 edition. Beat 4 is kept as F-sharp.
	WW	224		The 2016 edition removes *dim.* in the WW as notated in the ballet. 1945 suite marked "*non dim.*" *Diminuendo* in the Brass only.
	Tutti	227, 228		Per ballet, Tutti *diminuendo*, as corrected in the 1989 edition.
?	Tutti	238	5	Piano reduction: Cb, Eb, Gb, C; Ballet: B, Eb, Gb, C; 1919: B, E-nat., G-nat., B-nat., C-nat.; 1945: B, G, D, F, C. Conductor decision
				Berceuse
	Harp	16 & 20	4	Pitches in the gliss. notated as in the ballet.
	Flute	25 - 40		Notated for 2nd Flute in the original 1919 part but 1st Flute in the score. Notated for 1st Flute in the ballet, 1945 and 2016 edition.
!	Bsn. I	28	2	The controversial note D-nat. is correct as confirmed by the research from Jeffrey Lyman[6.]
!	Violin II	40	1	F-nat. in the Chester score. E-nat. notated in the 1919 Chester part and ballet Reh. 195 measure 5 and 2016 edition.
				Finale
	Harp	65 - end		Pitches changed from B major to C-flat major for better resonance.
	Tutti	98	1	*Sub.* **pp** for one measure. The *crescendo* starts in measure 99 per the 1945 and 1989 editions.

[6] D or D-flat? *Stravinsky's Berceuse and the Long Story of a Short Note* by Jeffrey Lyman, Ann Arbor, Michigan. Scan of measure 28 in the manuscript. <http://www-personal.umich.edu/~jlym/media/DorD%20flat.pdf>

Clinton F. Nieweg and Clark McAlister, August 2016

ORCHESTRA

2 Flutes

(2nd also Piccolo)

2 Oboes

(2nd also English Horn)

2 Clarinets (A)

2 Bassoons

4 Horns (F)

2 Trumpets (C)

3 Trombones

Tuba

Timpani

Percussion (3 players)

Tambourine, Triangle, Xylophone

Cymbals (suspended and crash), Bass Drum

Harp

Piano (also Celesta)

Violin I

Violin II

Viola

Violoncello

Double Bass

Duration: ca.23 minutes

Premiere: April 12, 1919

Geneva, Victoria Hall

Orchestre de la Suisse Romande, Ernest Ansermet (conductor)

THE FIREBIRD
Suite from the Ballet
Re-orchestrated by the composer 1919

IGOR STRAVINSKY

Introduction

Edited by Clark McAlister & Clinton F. Nieweg

♪ = 108

Flute 1-2 (2=Piccolo)

Oboe 1-2 (2=English Horn)

Clarinet 1-2 in A*

Bassoon 1-2

1-2 Horn in F

3-4

Trumpet 1-2 in C*

1-2 Trombone   TACET

3   TACET

Tuba

Timpani

Tambourine   TACET

Triangle   TACET

Cymbals   TACET

Bass Drum   *pp*   TACET

Xylophone

Piano and Celeste

Harp

♪ = 108

1 Violin

2

Viola   *muted*   *pp*

Violoncello   *muted*   *pp*

Double Bass   *2 players, pizz, not muted*   *pp*   *altri, arco, muted*   *pp*

* Set includes parts in B♭.

4
5
soli
ppp
Tbn.
B.D.
Vn.
Va.
Vc.
D.B.
7
Cl.
p
pp subito
Bsn.
pp
ppp
Hn.
Tpt.
muted
(a little louder than the clarinets)
mp
mute out
Harp
gliss.
muted
sul tasto
2 players
soli, pizz

9
1
Cl.
2
1
Bsn.
2
2
Hn.
4
1
Tbn.
2
B.D.
9
1
Vn.
2
Va.
Vc.
D.B.
ord.
mutes off
mutes off
2 players, pizz.
others, arco
11
1
Fl.
2
Flute
1
Cl.
2
1
Bsn.
2
1
Vn.
2
Va.
Vc.
D.B.

* By sliding the finger along the string indicated, the harmonics indicated are produced automatically.

* English Horn cued in Ob. 2 part.

L'oiseau de feu et sa danse

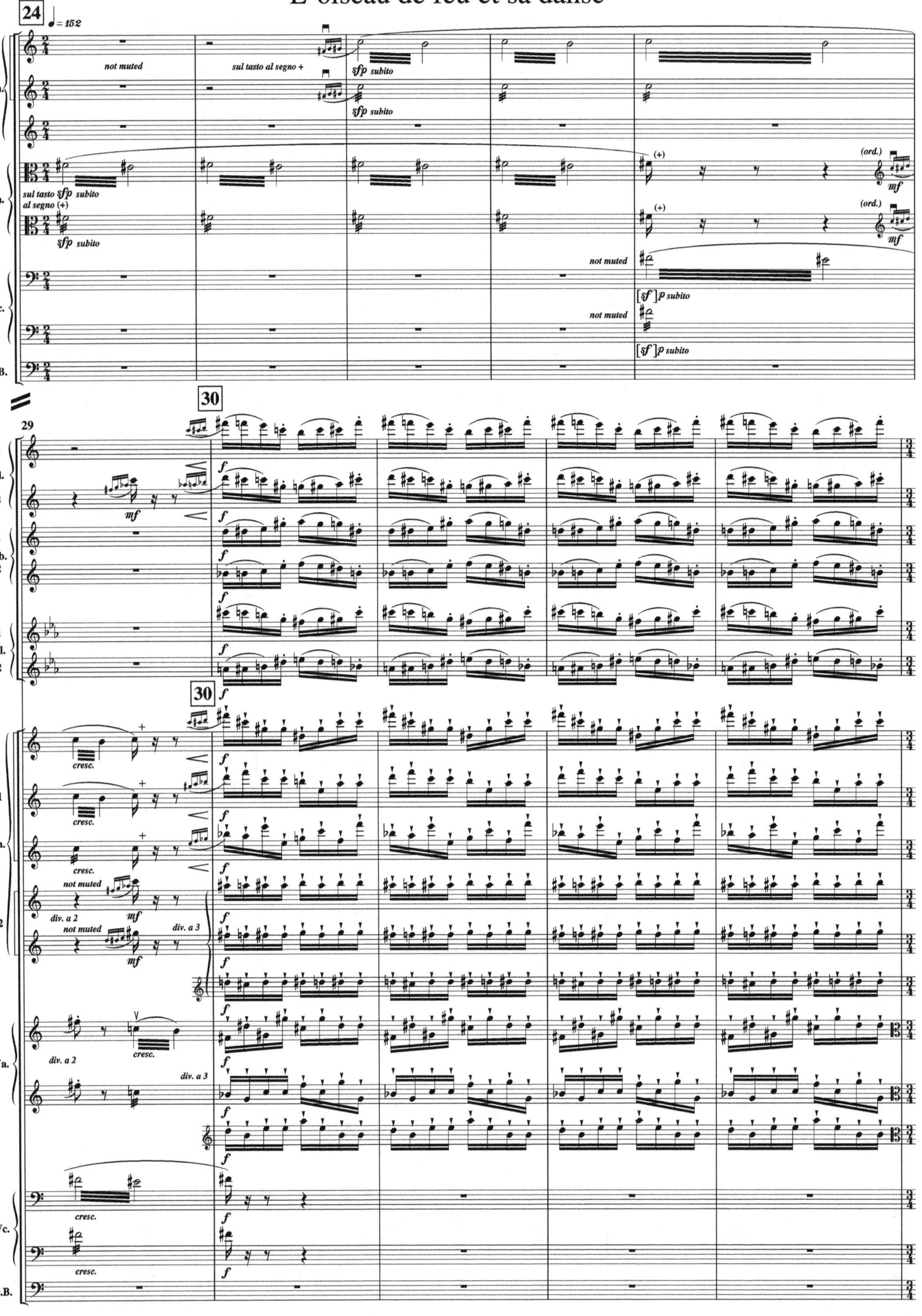

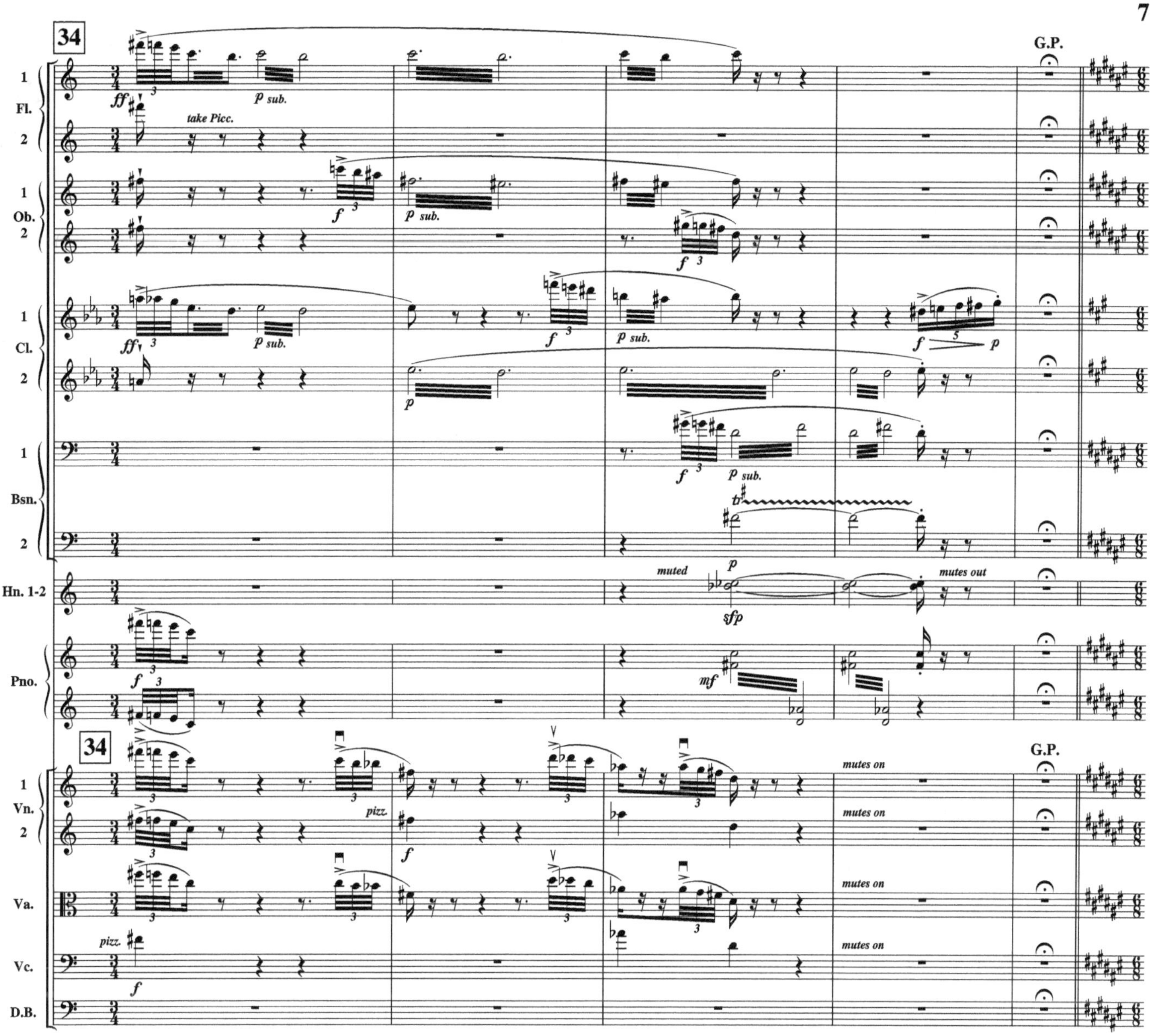

Variation de l'oiseau de feu

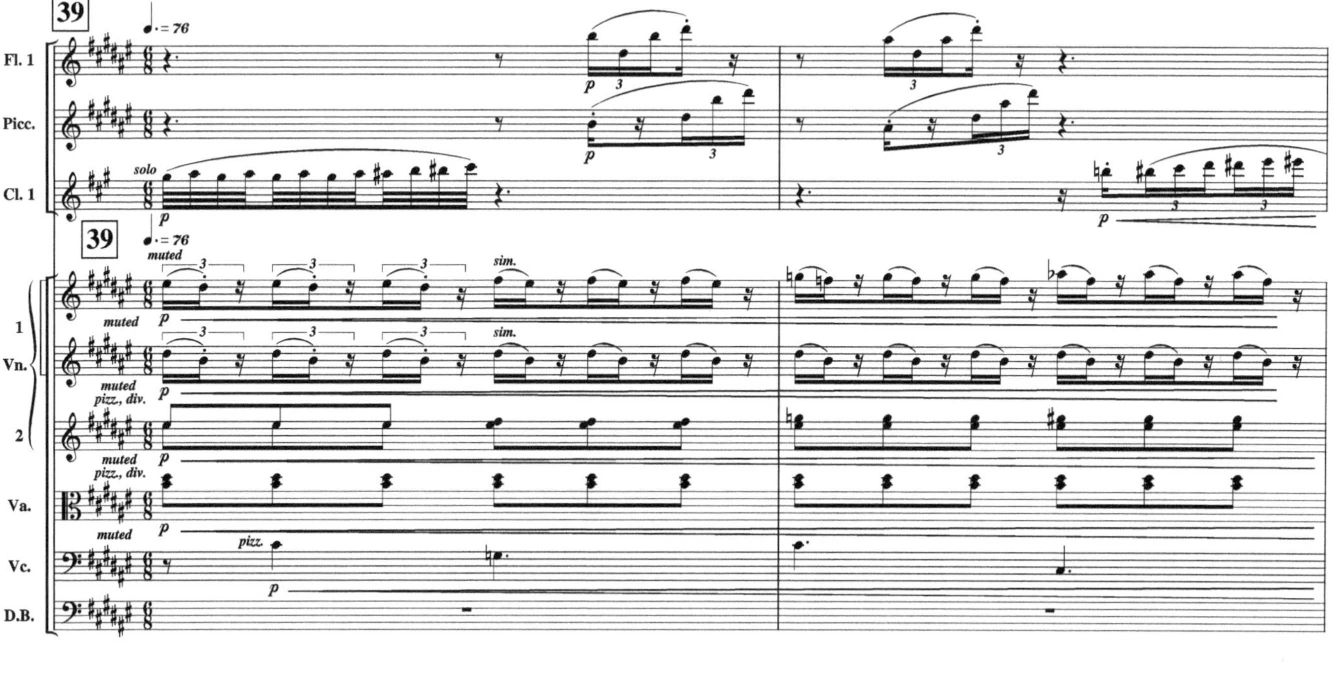

41
43
Fl. 1
Picc.
Cl. 1
Bsn. 1
Pno.
Vn.
1
2
Va.
Vc.
D.B.
mf
p
sf - mf
sim.
div. a 3
div. a 2
arco
pizz.
44
Ob. 1
a 3

47
Fl. 1
Picc.
1
Cl.
2
Bsn.
1-2
Hn.
3-4
Pno.
Harp
47
1
Vn.
2
Va.
Vc.
D.B.
mf
p
f
tr
gliss. on the white keys
gliss. on the white keys
9
jeté
leggero
molto
retrouvez
arco
pizz.
div. a 2
sf secco
sf

50
52
Fl. 1
Picc.
1
Cl.
2
Bsn. 1
1-2
Hn.
3-4
gliss. on the white keys
Pno.
Harp
jeté
tr
molto
pizz.
arco
très sec
Vn.
Va.
Vc.
D.B.
mf secco

53
Fl. 1
Picc.
Ob.
Cl.
1
2
Hn. 1-2
Tpt. 1-2
Pno.
Harp
Vn.
Va.
Vc.
D.B.
muted
2. mute in
tu tu
arco, jeté
arco
pizz.
sf étouffez
gliss.
sff
ff
mf
mp
p
f

56
Fl. 1
Picc.
Ob.
1
Cl.
2
1-2
Hn.
3-4
Tpt. 1-2
Pno.
Harp
Vn.
1
2
Va.
Vc.
D.B.
mf
f
sff
p
ff
3. muted
2. muted
8va
sf etouffez
gliss.
pizz.
arco, jeté
arco
arco au talon
très sec et très fort

59
60
Fl. 1
Picc.
1
Cl.
2
Pno.
Harp
Vn.
Va.
Vc.
D.B.
gliss. on the white keys
gliss.
8va
div.
sim.
III. pos.
pizz.
arco
div. pizz.
f
ff
sff
mf
mp
p
62
64
Bsn. 1
Cl. 1
div. a 3
div. a 2
sf - mf
tr

65
Fl. 1
Picc.
Cl. 1
Bsn. 1
Pno.
Vn.
1
2
Va.
Vc.
D.B.
mf
p
tr
sf-mf
div. a 3
arco
68
p sempre cresc.
sim.
div. a 2
pizz.

71
72
Fl. 1
Picc.
Ob.
Cl.
Bsn.
Pno.
Harp
Vn.
Va.
Vc.
D.B.
leggero
gliss. on the white keys
gliss. C maj.
jeté
arco
pizz.
arco, muted
mutes off

74
Fl. 1
Picc.
Ob. 1
Ob. 2
Cl. 1
Cl. 2
Hn. 1
Pno.
Vn. 1
Vn. 2
Va.
Vc.
D.B.
tr
open
f
ff
arco
reprenez l'archet

76
77
Fl. 1
Picc.
Ob.
Cl.
Hn. 1
Pno.
Vn.
Va.
Vc.
D.B.
t k t
sim.
mp
mp sub.
f
p
p sub.
II. pos. sul D
pizz.
tr
8va

79
Fl. 1
Picc.
Ob.
Cl.
Hn. 1
Tpt.
Pno.
Harp
Vn.
Va.
Vc.
D.B.
tr
p sub.
take Fl. 2
mf
p
ff
open
RH
gliss. on the white keys
l.v.
f
sautillé
solo – mute off
pizz.
arco non arpeg.
arco
not muted

Ronde des princesses

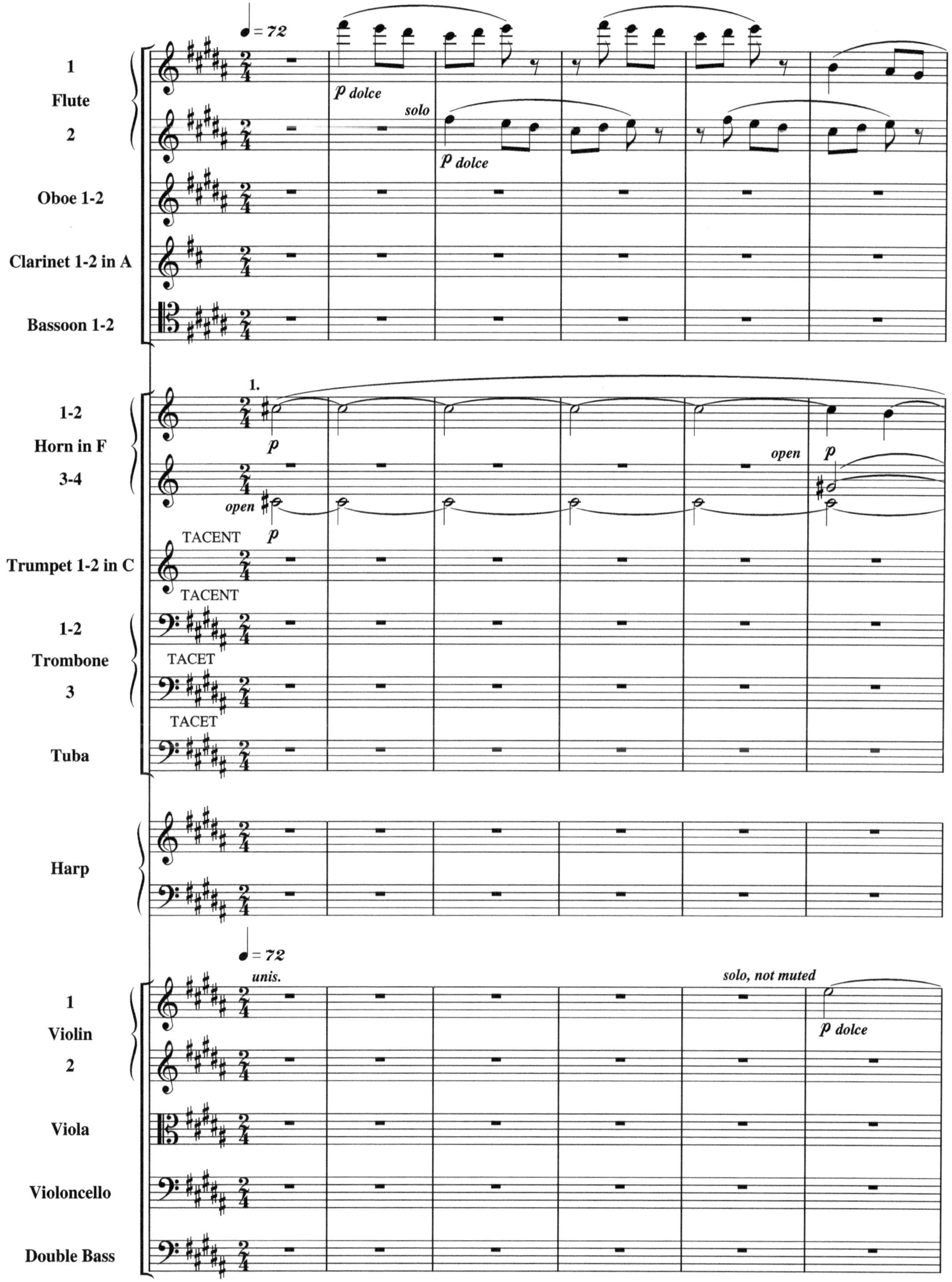

8
poco ritard.
a tempo (♩= 72)
Fl.
Ob.
1. solo
mf
1-2
Hn.
3-4
Harp
Vn.
Va.
Vc.
D.B.
tutti, muted
(muted)
p
solo, not muted
p dolce e
12
Cl.
Bsn.
2. mf
mf dolce
mp
pp
3.
cantabile
solo – mute on
pizz.

17
♩= 92
Bsn.
Vn.
Va.
Vc.
D.B.
(muted)
muted
tutti, div.
e subito pp
sim.
molto
25
Cl.
poco
pp sempre
arco, muted
33
1. solo
p dolce
Hn. 1-2
unis.

41
poco rall.
Poco meno mosso
rallent.
Fl.
Ob.
Cl.
Bsn.
Hn. 1-2
(1.)
Vn.
Va.
Vc.
D.B.
47
♩= 72
1. solo
Harp
solo, not muted
dolce e
51
1. solo
mp dolce
cantabile
solo mute on
(muted) pizz.

56
♩= 92
Fl.
Hn. 1-2
Hn. 3-4
1. solo
p dolce
solo
4.
ppp
Vn. 1
Vn. 2
Va.
Vc.
D.B.
tutti
div., pizz.
muted
div., pizz.
unis.
arco
poco
64
1. solo
pp sub.
div.
unis.
pizz.
arco, not muted
72
Ob. 1
Ob. 2
Cl.
Bsn.
mf
p dolce
pp

80
Fl.
Ob.
Cl.
Harp
solo
p
1.
2. p
p sons étouffes
Laissez vibrer
80
1
Vn.
2
Va.
Vc.
D.B.
pp tremolo
pp tremolo
88
rit.
a tempo
Fl. 2 take Picc.
f sub.
f
p dolce
Bsn.
1-2
Hn.
3-4
mf
p
88
div.
solo, not muted
solo mute in
(not muted)
mf

96
rall.
Ob.
mp
dim.
1-2
Hn.
3-4
Harp
solo
p
Vn.
1
2
4 players
dolcissimo
unis.
div.
sur la touche
Va.
pp
tutti, muted
Vc.
D.B.
104
Lento ♩= 58 (environ)
110
Picc.
solo
ppp
1. solo
Cl.
Hn. 1-2
pp
tutti, div.
sempre pp sino al fine
mutes off

113
Fl.
Ob.
pp
Cl.
(1.)
pp
3
Bsn.
(1.)
1-2
Hn.
3-4
pp
3
Tpt.
1-2
Tbn.
3
Tuba
Harp
8va
mutes off
1
Vn.
2
Va.
unis., not muted
pp
Vc.
D.B.

Danse infernale du roi Kastcheï

5
Fl. 1
Picc.
Ob.
Cl.
Bsn.
mf
f
mf
f
1-2
Hn.
3-4
1. mf
f
Tpt.
1-2
Tbn.
3
Tuba
Timp.
B.D.
Xylo.
Pno.
Harp
1
Vn.
2
Va.
Vc.
D.B.

9
11
Fl. 1
Picc.
Ob.
Cl.
Bsn.
Hn. 1-2
Hn. 3-4
Tpt.
Tbn. 1-2
Tbn. 3
Tuba
Timp.
B.D.
Xylo.
Pno.
Harp
Vn. 1
Vn. 2
Va.
Vc.
D.B.
soli
mf
sfff
f
pp subito
8va
11

13
Fl. 1
Picc.
Ob.
Cl.
Bsn.
1-2
Hn.
3-4
Tpt.
1-2
Tbn.
3
Tuba
Timp.
B.D.
Xylo.
Pno.
Harp
1
Vn.
2
Va.
Vc.
D.B.
sfff
mf
f
mf < f
pp subito
8va

17
19
Fl. 1
Picc.
Ob.
Cl.
Bsn.
1-2
Hn.
3-4
Tpt.
1-2
Tbn.
3
Tuba
Timp.
B.D.
Xylo.
Pno.
Harp
1
Vn.
2
Va.
Vc.
D.B.
sfff
mf subito
sf
mf
2. solo
a 2
f
pp subito
p subito
8va

21
Fl. 1
Picc.
Ob.
Cl.
Bsn.
Hn. 1-2
Hn. 3-4
Tpt.
Tbn. 1-2
Tbn. 3
Tuba
Timp.
B.D.
Xylo.
Pno.
Harp
Vn. 1
Vn. 2
Va.
Vc.
D.B.
sfff
f
pp subito
p subito
8va

25
27
Fl. 1
Picc.
Ob.
Cl.
Bsn.
1-2
Hn.
3-4
Tpt.
1-2
Tbn.
3
Tuba
Timp.
B.D.
Xylo.
Pno.
Harp
Vn.
1
2
Va.
Vc.
D.B.
a 2
1.
non div.
pizz.
div.
sempre
8va
sfff
sf
f
ff
fff

30
Fl. 1
Picc.
Ob.
Cl.
Bsn.
1-2
Hn.
3-4
Tpt.
1-2
Tbn.
3
Tuba
Timp.
B.D.
Xylo.
Pno.
Harp
Vn.
Va.
Vc.
D.B.
sf
f
sf sempre
1.
2.
pp
8va
très court e fort
sff
très fort en sons étouffés
mp
(pizz.)

35
39
Fl. 1
Picc.
take Flute
Ob.
Cl.
Bsn.
1-2
Hn.
3-4
poco
Tpt.
muted
1-2
Tbn.
3
Tuba
Timp.
B.D.
Xylo.
Pno.
Harp
RH
1
Vn.
2
Va.
Vc.
D.B.
arco
(pizz.)
fff
ff
f
mf
p

41
Fl. 1 2
Cl.
Hn. 1-2
Tpt.
Vn. 1 2
Va.
Vc.
D.B.
mf
p poco
2. mf
46
47
Fl. 1 2
Ob.
Cl.
Hn. 1-2
Tpt.
Pno.
Harp
Vn. 1 2
Va.
Vc.
D.B.
f sons etouffés
jeté
arco jeté
(pizz.)
f
mf

51
55
Fl.
Ob.
Cl.
a 2
Bsn.
Hn.
solo
sempre poco sf
Pno.
Harp
Vn.
Va.
Vc.
pizz.
D.B.
56
sempre sf
at the frog
arco

59
Fl.
1
2
Ob.
Cl.
Bsn.
1-2
Hn.
3-4
Tpt.
1. solo
a 2
2.
59
non arp.
Vn.
ben marcato
Va.
Vc.
pizz.
(pizz.)
D.B.
63
Fl. 2 take Picc.
sempre
3
Pno.
Harp
non div.
col legno
div., pizz.
ord.
marcatissimo

67
Fl. 1
Picc.
1
Ob.
2
1
Cl.
2
Bsn.
1-2
Hn.
3-4
Tpt.
1-2
Tbn.
3
Tuba
Timp.
B.D.
Xylo.
Pno.
Harp
1
Vn.
2
Va.
Vc.
D.B.
ff
f
sf sempre
1. open
8va
arco
col legno
div., pizz.
pizz.
sempre f

71
73
Fl. 1
Picc.
1
Ob.
2
1
Cl.
2
Bsn.
a 2
1-2
Hn.
3-4
Tpt.
1-2
Tbn.
3
Tuba
2. open
open
Timp.
wood sticks
B.D.
Xylo.
(8va)
Pno.
Harp
1
Vn.
2
Va.
Vc.
D.B.
non arpegg.
unis., arco
arco
mf
f
ff
sff
sff très sec

75
Ob.
Cl.
Bsn.
Hn. 1-2
Tpt.
Xylo.
Pno.
1 Vn. 2
Va.
Vc.
D.B.
sf très sec
1. bouché-cuivré
poco sf
1. solo
pizz.
79
Fl. 1
Picc.
div.
unis.

83
85
Fl. 1
Picc.
Ob.
Cl.
Bsn.
1-2 Hn. 3-4
Tpt.
1-2 Tbn. 3
Tuba
Timp.
B.D.
Xylo.
Pno.
Harp
1 Vn. 2
Va.
Vc.
D.B.
sf
tr
f
1. bouché-cuivré
poco sf
1.
1., gliss.
pos. VI I VII
gliss.
mf
6
3

86
Fl. 1
Picc.
Ob.
1 Cl. 2
Bsn.
Hn. 3-4
Tpt.
Tbn. 1-2
f (gliss.)
1 Vn. 2
Va.
Vc.
D.B.
tr
3.
mp
88
bouchés-cuivrés
Xylo.
Pno.

91
Fl. 1
Picc.
Ob.
1 Cl. 2
Bsn.
1-2 Hn. 3-4
Tpt.
1-2 Tbn. 3
Tuba
Timp.
B.D.
Xylo.
Pno.
Harp
1 Vn. 2
Va.
Vc.
D.B.
solo
open
bouché-cuivré
1. muted
muted
arco
più f
gliss.
8va
ff
sff
mf

95
Fl. 1
Picc.
Ob.
Cl.
Bsn.
Hn.
Tpt.
Tbn.
Tuba
Timp.
B.D.
Xylo.
Pno.
Harp
Vn.
Va.
Vc.
D.B.
2. open
1. mute out
2. (open)
open
Timpani mallet
8va
div.
sub. mf (non cresc.)
gliss.

99
Fl. 1
Ob.
Cl.
Bsn.
1.
99
unis.
Vn.
unis.
Va.
one player
Vc.
altri
D.B.
103
Fl. 1
Picc.
Ob.
Cl.
Bsn.
Hn. 1-2
Vn.
Va.
Vc.
D.B.

107
Fl. 1
Ob.
Cl.
Bsn.
Hn. 1-2
1. solo
107
1
Vn.
2
Va.
Vc.
unis.
D.B.
111
Fl. 1
Ob.
Cl.
Bsn.
Hn. 1-2
1
Vn.
2
Va.
Vc.
D.B.

115
Fl. 1
Picc.
Ob.
Cl.
Bsn.
1-2
Hn.
3-4
Harp
gliss.
Vn.
Va.
Vc.
D.B.
div.
pizz.
120
123
unis., pizz.
pizz.

125
Fl. 1
Picc.
Ob.
Cl.
Bsn.
1-2
Hn.
3-4
Tpt.
1-2
Tbn.
3
Tuba
Timp.
B.D.
Xylo.
Pno.
Harp
1
Vn.
2
Va.
Vc.
D.B.
mf
f
f (non dim.)
ff
sf
più f
mp
mf
arco
(pizz.)

129
Fl. 1
Picc.
1
Ob.
2
1
Cl.
2
Bsn.
1-2
Hn.
3-4
Tpt.
1-2
Tbn.
3
Tuba
Timp.
B.D.
Xylo.
Pno.
Harp
1
Vn.
2
Va.
Vc.
D.B.
ff
f
mf
tr
3
open
1. open
3. non dim.
glissando on the white keys
m.d.
(𝄾)
arco

134
135
Fl. 1
Picc.
1
Ob.
2
1
Cl.
2
Bsn.
1-2
Hn.
3-4
Tpt.
1-2
Tbn.
3
Tuba
Timp.
B.D.
Xylo.
Pno.
Harp
1. non dim.
4. non dim.
135
1
Vn.
2
Va.
Vc.
D.B.

139
Fl. 1
Picc.
1
Ob.
2
1
Cl.
2
f
ff
tr
Bsn.
1. non dim.
1-2
Hn.
3-4
4. non dim.
1
Tpt.
2
1-2
Tbn.
3
Tuba
Timp.
mf
B.D.
Xylo.
Pno.
Harp
1
Vn.
2
Va.
Vc.
D.B.

143
Fl. 1
Picc.
Ob.
Cl.
Bsn.
1-2
Hn.
3-4
Tpt.
1-2
Tbn.
3
Tuba
Timp.
Tamb.
Trgl.
Cym.
B.D.
Xylo.
Pno.
Harp
143
1
Vn.
2
Va.
Vc.
D.B.
mf
sfff
p
3.
sff
fff
p subito
pp
pizz.

149
151
Fl. 1
Picc.
Ob.
Cl.
Bsn.
1-2
Hn.
3-4
Tpt.
1-2
Tbn.
3
Tuba
Timp.
Tamb.
Trgl.
Cym.
B.D.
Xylo.
Pno.
Harp
1
Vn.
2
Va.
Vc.
D.B.
soli
soli
mf
f
p

155
159
Fl. 1
Picc.
Ob.
a 2
1
Cl.
2
Bsn.
1-2
Hn.
3-4
soli
Tpt.
2. solo
1. solo
muted
ff marcatiss.
1-2
Tbn.
3
Tuba
Timp.
Tamb.
Trgl.
Cym.
B.D.
Xylo.
Pno.
8va
Harp
1
Vn.
2
Va.
Vc.
D.B.
arco

161
165
Fl. 1
Picc.
Ob.
a 2
1
Cl.
2
Bsn.
1-2
Hn.
3-4
2.
Tpt.
1. solo
ff marcatissimo
1-2
Tbn.
3
Tuba
Timp.
Tamb.
Trgl.
Cym.
B.D.
Xylo.
8va
Pno.
f sempre
Harp
f sempre
pizz.
1
Vn.
2
Va.
Vc.
D.B.

167
Fl. 1
Picc.
Ob.
Cl.
Bsn.
1-2
Hn.
3-4
Tpt.
1-2
Tbn.
3
Tuba
Timp.
Tamb.
Trgl.
Cym.
B.D.
Xylo.
Pno.
Harp
1
Vn.
2
Va.
Vc.
D.B.
f
sf
sf sempre
sff
pp
très court et fort
très fort et sons étouffés
div.
unis.
mp
pizz.

173
177
Fl. 1
Picc.
Ob.
Cl.
Bsn.
ff
f staccatissimo (très sec)
2.
p
1-2
Hn.
3-4
3.
Tpt.
1. open
ff très court
1-2
Tbn.
3
Tuba
Timp.
Tamb.
Trgl.
Cym.
B.D.
Xylo.
with triangle beater
Pno.
mf
Harp
1
Vn.
2
arco
sf
Va.
two players, pizz.
altri, arco
one player, pizz
Vc.
D.B.
pizz.
f

179
183
Fl. 1
Picc.
Ob.
Cl.
1
Bsn.
2
1-2
Hn.
3-4
Tpt.
1-2
Tbn.
3
Tuba
Timp.
Tamb.
Trgl.
Cym.
B.D.
Xylo.
Pno.
Harp
1
Vn.
2
Va.
Vc.
D.B.
solo
f
mf
4. p
pizz.
p
arco
non div.
poco più f
arco, div.
sf
sim.
one player, pizz.
altri, arco
sempre sim.

184
accelerando poco a poco
Fl. 1
Picc.
Ob.
Cl.
a 2
1
Bsn.
2
1-2
Hn.
3-4
Tpt.
1-2
Tbn.
3
Tuba
Timp.
Tamb.
Trgl.
Cym.
B.D.
Xylo.
Pno.
Harp
accelerando poco a poco
arco, div.
1
Vn.
2
Va.
Vc.
D.B.
sim.

189
193
Più mosso
Fl. 1
Picc.
Ob.
Cl.
Bsn.
(1.)
a 2
Hn.
1-2
3-4
Tpt.
sempre f
Tbn.
1-2
3
Tuba
Timp.
thumb roll
Tamb.
Trgl.
Cym.
B.D.
Xylo.
Pno.
Harp
Vn.
1
2
unis.
div.
arco
tutti, unis.
Va.
Vc.
D.B.
pizz.

194
Fl. 1
Picc.
Ob.
Cl.
Bsn.
1-2
Hn.
3-4
1
Tpt.
2
1-2
Tbn.
3
Tuba
Timp.
Tamb.
Trgl.
Cym.
B.D.
Xylo.
Pno.
Harp
1
Vn.
2
Va.
Vc.
D.B.
f
p
sff
pizz.
arco
div.

201
Fl. 1
Picc.
Ob.
Cl.
Bsn.
1-2
Hn.
3-4
Tpt.
1-2
Tbn.
3
Tuba
Timp.
Tamb.
Trgl.
Cym.
B.D.
Xylo.
Pno.
Harp
sf sempre
sff
sf
201
arco
très fort
sim.
1
Vn.
2
Va.
Vc.
D.B.

208
209
Fl. 1
Picc.
1
Ob.
2
Cl.
Bsn.
1-2
Hn.
3-4
Tpt.
1-2
Tbn.
3
Tuba
Timp.
Tamb.
Trgl.
Cym.
B.D.
Xylo.
Pno.
Harp
1
Vn.
2
Va.
Vc.
D.B.
sempre ff
più sf
très fort
sff
fff
sfff
sempre fff

213
215
Fl. 1
Picc.
Ob.
1
2
Cl.
Bsn.
1-2
Hn.
3-4
Tpt.
1-2
Tbn.
3
Tuba
sfff
Timp.
Tamb.
Trgl.
Cym.
B.D.
Xylo.
Pno.
Harp
215
Vn.
1
2
Va.
Vc.
D.B.

217
Fl. 1
Picc.
1
Ob.
2
Cl.
Bsn.
1-2
Hn.
3-4
Tpt.
1-2
Tbn.
3
Tuba
Timp.
Tamb.
Trgl.
Cym.
B.D.
Xylo.
Pno.
Harp
1
Vn.
2
Va.
Vc.
D.B.
tr
sfff

221
Fl. 1
Picc.
Ob.
Cl.
Bsn.
1-2
Hn.
3-4
Tpt.
1-2
Tbn.
3
Tuba
Timp.
Tamb.
Trgl.
Cym.
B.D.
Xylo.
Pno.
Harp
221
1
Vn.
2
Va.
Vc.
D.B.
ff
fff
a 2
1.
2.
non dim.
soft sticks
f
gliss. on the white keys
8va
gliss.
div. a 3
tr

68

* The low C should be played by the Basses who have it.

229
Ob.
1
Bsn.
2
1.
p
Vn.
p e staccato
div.
pizz.
Va.
Vc.
D.B.
234
235
Fl. 1
mf staccato
cresc.
Cl.
Hn. 1-2
mp
mf
arco
pizz.

239
[o· = d·]
Fl. 1
Picc.
Ob.
Cl.
Bsn.
1-2
Hn.
3-4
Tpt.
1-2
Tbn.
3
Tuba
Timp.
Tamb.
Trgl.
(soft sticks)
tremolo
Cym.
B.D.
Xylo.
Pno.
Harp
239
[o· = d·]
1
Vn.
2
Va.
Vc.
D.B.
mf
p
pp
legatissimo
unis.
arco
très sec

245
247
Fl. 1
Picc.
Ob.
Cl.
Bsn.
1-2
Hn.
3-4
Tpt.
1-2
Tbn.
3
Tuba
Timp.
Tamb.
Trgl.
Cym.
B.D.
Xylo.
Pno.
Harp
Vn.
Va.
Vc.
D.B.
wood sticks
très fort
sul LA
non div.

251
255
Fl. 1
Picc.
Ob.
Cl.
Bsn.
Hn.
Tpt.
Tbn.
Tuba
Timp. sticks
Timp.
Tamb.
Trgl.
Cym.
B.D.
Xylo.
gliss. on the white keys
m.d.
Pno.
Harp
gliss.
Vn.
Va.
Vc.
D.B.
sim.

pour finir
pour enchaîner
258
259
Andante ♩ = 60
Fl. 1
Picc.
take Flute
Ob.
p subito
Cl.
fff
1.
p
Bsn.
Hn. 1-2
Hn. 3-4
(1.) p
2. p subito
2. p
Tpt.
Tbn. 1-2
Tbn. 3
Tuba
Timp.
Tamb.
Trgl.
l.v.
Cym.
B.D.
Xylo.
8va
Pno.
to Celesta
Harp
non arpeg.
Vn. 1
Vn. 2
Va.
div., muted
Vc.
D.B.

Berceuse

Andante ♩= 60
3
Flute 1-2
Oboe 1-2
Clarinet 1-2 in A
1. solo
Bassoon 1-2
p
1-2
Horn in F
3-4
Trumpet 1-2 in C
1-2
Trombone
3
Tuba
Timpani
Triangle
Bass Drum
Celesta
(Piano optional)
Harp
p
Andante ♩= 60
3
1
Violin
2
second half (muted)
Viola
p
unis. (muted)
Violoncello
pp
second half
div., pizz.
Double Bass
pp

Ob.
Bsn.
Harp
Vn.
Va.
Vc.
D.B.
1. solo
div., muted
muted
pizz., muted
tutti, div.
div. a 4
pizz.
div.
arco
mute on
solo (not muted)
mf cantabile
poco meno f

17
21
1
Fl.
2
Ob.
Cl.
Bsn.
a 2
1-2
Hn.
3-4
Tpt.
1-2
Tbn.
3
Tuba
Timp.
Trgl.
B.D.
Cel.
Harp
Vn.
Va.
Vc.
D.B.
mf espress.
p flautando al segno (+)
tutti, div.
arco
div., pizz.

23
rit.
25
a tempo
Fl.
Ob.
Cl.
Bsn.
1. solo
Hn.
Tpt.
Tbn.
Tuba
Timp.
Trgl.
B.D.
Cel. *
Harp
Vn.
Va.
Vc.
solo
ten.
others (second half)
D.B.
div.

* or Piano 8va.

28
29
Fl.
Bsn.
Harp
(8va)
29
1
Vn.
2
pp
pp
Va.
Vc.
(second half, div.)
D.B.
pp
33
1.
Ob.
pp
più pp
niente
Harp
laissez vibrer
laissez vibrer
33
36
sul tasto sino al segno (+)
1
pp
Vn.
sul tasto sino al segno (+)
pp
sul tasto sino al segno (+)
2
pp
sul tasto sino al segno (+)
Va.
sul tasto sino al segno (+)
sul tasto sino al segno (+)
Vc.
others
sul tasto
(muted)
D.B.
(muted) pp
div. a 3
pp

41
Vn. 1
Vn. 2
Va.
Vc.
D.B.
(+) mutes off
tutti, div.
sul tasto sino al segno (+)
mutes off
sul tasto
div.
Final
47
Lento maestoso 𝅗𝅥 = 54
1. solo
Hn. 1-2
p dolce e cantabile
unis.
not muted
not muted
unis., not muted
53
55
Fl.
Cl.
Hn. 1-2
Harp
gliss.
p dolce
pp
unis., not muted

59
1
Fl.
2
cresc.
p cresc.
take Picc.
1
Ob.
2
p
cresc.
Cl.
1.
2. p
p cresc.
Bsn.
1-2
Hn.
3-4
Tpt.
1-2
Tbn.
3
Tuba
Timp.
Trgl.
B.D.
Pno.
Harp
59
1
Vn.
2
div.
10
12
sul SOL
tr
Va.
Vc.
pizz.
arco
D.B.

65
69
Fl. 1
Picc.
Ob.
Cl.
Bsn.
1-2
Hn.
3-4
Tpt.
1-2
Tbn.
3
Tuba
Timp.
Trgl.
B.D.
Pno.
Harp
1
Vn.
2
Va.
Vc.
D.B.
f
fff
ff
mf cresc.
f cresc.
a 2
gliss.
div. a 2
10
7
11
fff ben marcato
Vn. 2 div. a 3

71
73
Più mosso
Fl. 1
Picc.
Ob.
Cl.
Bsn.
1-2
Hn.
3-4
Tpt.
1-2
Tbn.
3
Tuba
Timp.
Trgl.
B.D.
Pno.
Harp
73
Più mosso
pp subito
poco a poco cresc.
mf cresc.
f cresc.
pp poco a poco cresc.
1
Vn.
2
Va.
Vc.
D.B.

* Glissando on harmonics; cued in Horn 2, 4.

83
Fl. 1
Picc.
Ob.
Cl.
Bsn.
Hn.
Tpt.
Tbn.
Tuba
Timp.
Trgl.
B.D.
Pno.
Harp
Vn.
Va.
Vc.
D.B.
fff
ff
ff marcatissimo
f
tr

85
Fl. 1
Picc.
Ob.
1
Cl.
2
Bsn.
1-2
Hn.
3-4
Tpt.
1-2
Tbn.
3
Tuba
Timp.
Trgl.
B.D.
Pno.
Harp
1
Vn.
2
Va.
Vc.
D.B.
div.

87
Doppio valore ♩ = 104 Maestoso
Fl. 1
Picc.
Ob.
a 2
Cl.
Bsn.
1-2
Hn.
3-4
Tpt.
1-2
Tbn.
3
Tuba
Timp.
Trgl.
B.D.
Pno.
Harp
sim.
87
Doppio valore ♩ = 104 Maestoso
1
Vn.
2
Va.
Vc.
D.B.
unis.
fff
ff

poco a poco allargando

poco a poco allargando

sempre più cresc.

93
Molto pesante 𝅗𝅥 = 60
Fl. 1
Picc.
Ob.
Cl.
Bsn.
1-2
Hn.
3-4
Tpt.
1-2
Tbn.
3
Tuba
Timp.
Trgl.
Cyms.
B.D.
Pno.
Harp
1
Vn.
2
Va.
Vc.
D.B.
ffff
sfff
fff
pp sub.
a 2

www.ingramcontent.com/pod-product-compliance
Lightning Source LLC
La Vergne TN
LVHW081319060426
835509LV00015B/1589